The Kids' Baseball Workout

A Fun Way to Get in Shape and Improve Your Game

Jeffrey B. Fuerst

Illustrations by
Anne Canevari Green

The Millbrook Press   Brookfield, Connecticut

**To Jake, for asking to have a catch.
And to Joel and Mark, for agreeing to one.**

Photographs courtesy of Sports Illustrated: p. 11 (© Jason Wise); SportsChrome: p. 14 (© Rob Tringali, Jr.); AP/Wide World Photos: pp. 22, 32, 56, 63 (all), 73; Archive Photos: p. 29 (© Reuters/Mike Blake); Corbis: p. 47 (© Reuters Newmedia, Inc.)

Illustrations © 2002 by Anne Canevari Green

Library of Congress Cataloging-in-Publication Data
Fuerst, Jeffrey B.
The kids' baseball workout : how to get in shape and improve your game /
Jeffrey B. Fuerst.
p. cm.
Includes bibliographical references and index.
ISBN 0-7613-2307-4 (lib. bdg.)
1. Baseball for children—Training. 2. Physical fitness for children. 3. Exercise for children. I. Title.
GV880.4 .F84 2002 796.357'2—dc21 2001042718

Published by The Millbrook Press, Inc.
2 Old New Milford Road
Brookfield, Connecticut 06804
www.millbrookpress.com

Contents

Acknowledgments

I would like to thank all the kids, ballplayers, and exercise mavens
who helped get this book into shape, especially Eli London,
Steve Siden, Juliette Soucie, and these coaches: Scott Cantor,
Pomona, New York; Vic Federico, Yonkers, New York; Jerry Helfand,
Minneapolis, Minnesota; Peter London, University Heights, Ohio;
John Macchia, Carmel, New York; and Jonathan Rosen, Edgemont, New York.
I would also like to thank my editor, Anita Holmes, for the at bat.

A Word of Caution

Before you go to a sports gym or camp, the trainers require you to get an okay from your doctor—to make sure that your heart, lungs, and body are up to the task. Before you begin your own baseball workout program, you should talk with your parents. Perhaps they'll want you to get checked out by your doctor. And they may want to supervise the exercises and drills when you do them the first time to make sure you're doing them correctly.

Introduction

If you've picked up this book, you love to play baseball—and you want to become a better ballplayer. How do you polish your skills and shine on the baseball diamond? Listen to your coaches and practice, of course. You'll also want to study the game. Learn its fine points and you'll get a mental edge on the competition. But to perform your best on the field, you need to be in your best physical condition.

When you're in shape, you're more likely to stretch a double into a triple . . . run down a long fly ball that saves the game . . . or smack one over the fence to lead your team to victory. That's where this book comes in.

Other books can show you technique: how to play better baseball. This book gives you a workout plan and practice tips that will help you become a faster, stronger, and smarter player. It also includes fun, skill-building drills that you can do by yourself or with a few friends. Most are designed to do in a backyard or school playground. Only a few require an actual ballfield. All you'll need is a bat, a glove, a few balls—and a positive attitude.

You may want to ask an adult to help you do the exercises the first time, but with this book, *you* are the coach. Learn at your own pace. Over time, you will develop into what baseball experts call "the complete" ballplayer—someone who can do it all: throw, run, hit for average, hit with power, and field.

What are you waiting for? Read on, grab your gear, and go for it!

Chapter One
Conditioning the Body and Mind

The score is tied 3 to 3 with two players on and two down in the seventh inning. The manager for the Boston Red Sox signals for his left-handed relief pitcher throwing in the bullpen. The manager for the New York Yankees tells his best right-handed pinch hitter to loosen up in the on-deck circle.

Pros wouldn't think of jumping into a game without warming up their muscles first. They know that baseball is a game of quick starts, abrupt stops, and explosive body movements. Swinging a bat . . . racing down the line . . . sprinting after a long fly . . . or pegging the ball across the diamond can tear or pull a tight or "cold" muscle.

Warm Up and Stretch

Warming up and stretching are an important part of a ballplayer's daily routine.

During warm-ups, the lungs and heart begin to work harder. As more oxygen and blood flow through the body, muscle temperatures actually go up! You breathe a little faster and may even sweat a bit.

The warm-up gets your body ready for a more strenuous workout to come. It also gets your "head" in the game. You begin to think about what you want to accomplish during the workout, or in the game. Meanwhile, your senses get accustomed to their surroundings and the tasks ahead.

After a few minutes of warming up, ballplayers spend a few more minutes doing stretching exercises. Regular stretching helps develop long, loose, flexible muscles.

"Muscles are like taffy," explains Coach Scott, a personal trainer and former professional ballplayer from Pomona, New York. "They stretch when warm. But if you try to stretch them when they're cold, they'll snap."

Loose and limber muscles are less likely to get injured, adds Juliette Soucie, a personal trainer from New York, New York. Besides, stretching makes your body feel good and can help you relax.

Warm Up

To warm up, take from 5 to 7 minutes to do one or more of these exercises. Stop when you begin to sweat and breathe heavily.

- Jog/fast walk
- Jump rope
- Ride an exercise bike
- Walk on a treadmill
- Aerobic dance

After the warm-up, sip water. Keep a water bottle handy throughout your workout, too.

General Stretching

After you've warmed up, take a few minutes to do these ten stretching exercises in the order listed. Relax and breathe comfortably during stretches. When you feel a slight pulling (tension) in the muscles being stretched, hold that position steady for the amount of time given (usually 10 to 30 seconds). Try not to "bounce" when stretching. Quick, jerking movements can strain your muscles.

1. **Sky Grabs** (Upper back, shoulders)
   Lift your arms over your head and reach high. Rise up on your toes. Hold for 15 seconds. Repeat.

2. **Cross-Chest Pull** (Shoulders, triceps)
   Bend your elbow and place your throwing hand on the opposite shoulder. With your other hand, grab your throwing arm just above the elbow and pull gently. Hold for 15 seconds. Switch arms and repeat.

3. **Reach Back (Chest, biceps)**
   Interlace your fingers behind your back. Extend your arms out behind you and lift up. Hold for 30 seconds.

4. **The Traffic Cop (Forearm, wrist)**
   Hold one arm out in front of your chest, palm up and out in the "stop" position. Grab the fingers of the "stop" hand with your other hand. Gently pull back the fingers. Hold for 10 seconds. Switch arms and repeat.

5. **Left Face, Right Face (Neck)**
   Turn your head to the left and hold it in that position for 10 seconds. Turn your head to the right and hold for 10 seconds. Lower your chin to your chest and hold for 10.

6. **Hip Twists (Hips, waist, lower back)**
   Put your hands on your hips, feet shoulder-width apart and facing forward. Keep your knees and hips facing forward and turn at the waist to your left. Hold for 15 seconds. Turn to the right and hold for 15 seconds.

7. **Hello Down There! (Waist, buttocks)**
   Put your hands on your hips, feet shoulder-width apart, knees bent slightly. Bend forward at the waist until you feel a pulling in your buttocks muscles. Hold for 10 seconds and repeat.

8. **The Stork (Quad)**
   Hold onto something with your left hand and shift your weight onto your left foot. Lift your right leg, bend it back at the knee, and grab the foot at the ankle with your right hand. Pull up until your heel touches your butt. Don't arch your back. Hold for 15 seconds. Switch legs.

9. The Walls of Jericho (Calf)

Place both hands at shoulder height against the side of a building, fence, or tree as if you're trying to hold it up. Move one foot back about 2 feet (.6 meters). Keep both feet on the ground and lean your body toward the wall, keeping the back knee straight. (The front knee can bend.) Hold for 15 seconds and repeat with your other leg.

10. The Can Opener (Hamstring)

Raise one leg onto a bench or fence and place it heel down, toes pointing up. Clasp your hands behind your back. Keep your legs straight and slowly bend at the waist. Bring your chest as close to your knee as you can. Hold for 30 seconds, then switch legs.

Cool Down and Stretch

After a tough workout you need to cool down your body, reduce your heart rate, and replace the fluids your body sweated out. Drink a glass of water and walk around for a few minutes until your breathing and heartbeat slow down to normal. Then, when you're relaxed, take a few minutes to stretch out those freshly exercised muscles.

During a workout, you jump, reach, sprint, and put your body through a lot of short pulling and pushing movements. This kind of exercise builds muscle strength and can make your muscles bigger. But the constant pushing and pulling also makes your muscles tighten up.

That's why it's just as important to stretch muscles *after* a workout as before. Doing a series of "cool down" stretches (you do them after you've cooled down a bit) will minimize next-day aches and pains. Postworkout stretching will help muscles retain some of that taffylike flexibility they gained during the workout.

Not stretching after a workout can lead to sore muscles and stiff joints and invites injury, says personal trainer Juliette Soucie. She strongly urges kids to get into the stretching habit. "Five minutes taken after a workout," she explains, "can save five days of sore muscles and help prevent five weeks of sitting on the bench later in the season when the overused muscles rebel."

Celebrity Profile

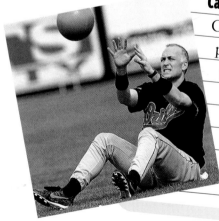

Cal "Iron Man" Ripken

Cal "Iron Man" Ripken could not have played a record-setting 2,632 consecutive games (16 years in a row!) if he had not kept himself in excellent shape. In the off-season, Cal cross-trained by playing basketball almost every day.

Cool Down

Cool-down exercises can be similar to warm-up exercises. Start with a few minutes of slow walking or jogging followed by stretching.

Targeted Stretching

Depending on the type of workout you've had, do at least a few of the following cool-down stretches that target some of the muscles you've just been using the most. All are done sitting or lying down.

1. **The Cannonball (Lower back)**
   Lie on your back, keeping your knees bent and your feet flat on the ground. Clasp your hands around your left knee and bring it to your chest. Hold for 15 seconds. Repeat with your right knee and hold for 15 seconds. Then pull both knees together and hold for 15 seconds.

2. **The Jackknife (Lower back, hamstring, calf muscles)**
   Lie on your back, legs straight, arms at your sides. Bend one leg, keeping your foot flat on the ground. Raise the other leg up as high as you can (to a 90-degree angle). Grab the raised leg with both hands at the ankle and pull toward you slightly. Point the toes of the raised leg toward you. Hold for 15 seconds. Switch legs and repeat.

3. Squinching Beauty (Quad)

Lie on the floor on your left side, head resting on your left arm extended straight out. Bend your right leg at the knee and grab the toes of your right foot with your right hand. Pull your right foot toward your buttocks. Hold for 30 seconds, then repeat with the other leg.

4. Body Scissors (Trunk, hips)

Lie on your back, arms straight out to the side. Lift one leg high, knee straight, and swing it over the other leg as far as you can without pulling your shoulder blades off the ground. Hold for 15 seconds, switch legs, and repeat.

5. Sitting Toe Touches (Hamstring)

Sit on the ground with your legs straight and feet about 6 inches (15 centimeters) apart. Slowly reach forward and touch the toes of your left foot. Hold for 15 seconds. Repeat, touching the toes of your right foot. Put both feet together and reach past your toes as far as you can. Hold again for 15 seconds.

6. Butterfly (Groin)

Sit on the ground and place the bottoms of your feet together. Grab your ankles with your hands and rest your elbows on your knees. Bend forward at the waist, gently pushing down on your knees with your elbows. Hold for 15 seconds. Repeat.

Workout Tip   Stay Active to Build Stamina

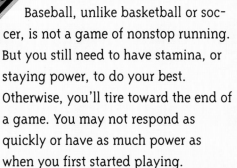

Baseball, unlike basketball or soccer, is not a game of nonstop running. But you still need to have stamina, or staying power, to do your best. Otherwise, you'll tire toward the end of a game. You may not respond as quickly or have as much power as when you first started playing.

To develop stamina, you must build up your heart and lung muscles. The more blood and oxygen the heart and lungs deliver to your muscles, the better they work. On days when you're not playing baseball, try running, swimming, cycling, in-line skating, jumping rope, or playing other sports like soccer and basketball. These "cross-training" activities will help you build heart-lung (aerobic) endurance. They may also build up some muscles not typically used in baseball, preventing injuries from overuse.

7. The Arrow (Back, shoulders, arms)

Lie on your back. Interlace your fingers and raise your arms over your head until they rest on the floor. Reach your fingers in the opposite direction of your toes. Hold for 15 seconds and repeat.

8. This Way, Thataway (Shoulders)

Extend one arm straight across your chest and grab it at the wrist with your other hand. Pull gently away from your body and hold for 15 seconds. Repeat with the other arm.

9. Finger Flex (Forearm, wrist)

Extend one arm straight across your chest, elbow bent slightly. Grab the fingers of the extended hand in the palm of the other. Push back gently. Hold for 15 seconds and switch arms.

Chapter Two
Throwing

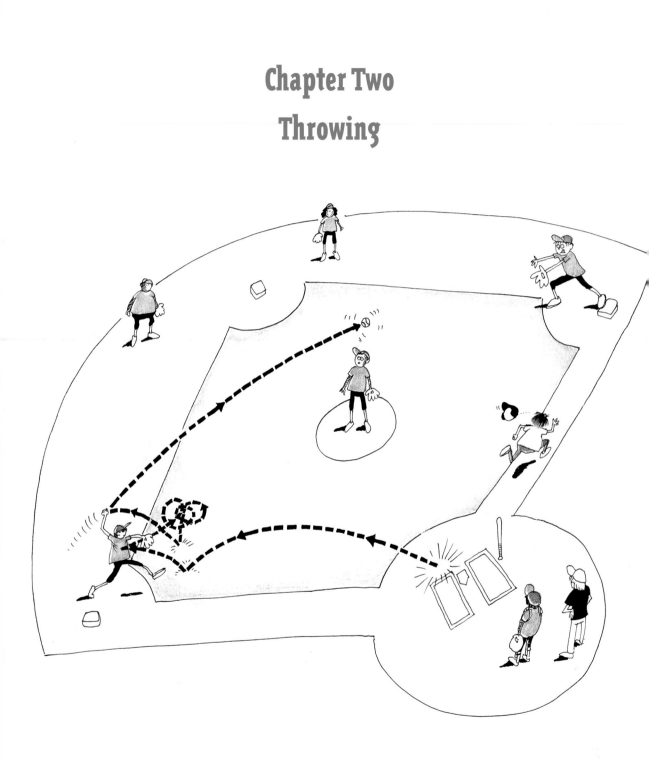

A wicked line drive nosedives in front of you at third. It short-hops over your glove and glances off your chest. You scramble for the spinning ball, pick it up with a handful of dirt, rear back, and fire a perfect strike into the first baseman's outstretched glove. The batter is out by a half step!

A strong, accurate throwing arm may be your most valuable asset. It's what gets players noticed at all levels, from Little League to high school and the Bigs. "Arm strength is a skill and one of the first things I look for in a player," says college scout Ken Lenihan. "Whether you are a pitcher or a position player, remember: Your arm is your future!" adds Gary Adams, head baseball coach at UCLA. "Make the time to take good care of it."

But you don't throw with your arm alone. It's a whole body affair! Your legs, of course, support your upper body and keep you balanced. They also provide power. Like a booster rocket, your legs give you the *oomph* you need to launch the ball. Your hips and trunk (back and stomach muscles) help turn your body into throwing position. Your shoulder muscles whip your arm back and forth. Your wrist snaps the ball to the plate.

How do all these body parts work together? See what happens when you

1. throw without moving your legs
2. throw without moving your back
3. throw without bending your elbow or snapping your wrist

Write down your observations on a piece of paper. Check your answers at the bottom of the page. To throw well, you need strong legs, flexibility in the waist and hips, a loose arm and wrist, and most important of all, a well-conditioned shoulder.

Warm Up and Stretch

Before you begin your throwing workout, always do from 10 to 15 minutes of warm-ups and stretching exercises (see chapter one).

Throwing Workout

Contrary to what you may think, gym teachers are not trying to torture you when they have you do strengthening exercises. These exercises are aimed at strengthening specific parts of your body that will help you throw better. (Groans optional.)

- Push-ups (Upper body)
  Lie on the ground, facedown. Place your hands, palms down, near your shoulders. Put your feet together and rise onto your toes. Then push up from the ground with your hands and arms until your elbows straighten. Keep your back and legs straight and fingers pointing forward. Lower your chest back toward the ground, but do not rest on the ground. Hold that position for a count of 2, then repeat 10 or more times.

ANSWERS: 1. You lose power. 2. You're awkward and stiff. 3. You lose control.

- **Wheelbarrow and Crab-Walk Races (Upper body)**
  More smile-friendly than push-ups, these exercises also strengthen your upper body.

  Wheelbarrow: Person A gets into position to do a push-up. Person B grabs Person A's legs around the thighs and lifts them waist high. Person A rises up on her hands and begins to move forward while Person B follows along. Walk for 20 feet (6 meters) or as far as possible without tipping over.

  Crabwalk: Sit on the ground, knees bent, feet flat, arms out to the side with your palms down. Raise your body off the ground so it is supported by your hands and legs. Walk 10 steps forward and 10 steps backward.

- **Crunchers (Stomach)**
  Lie on your back, knees bent, lower back flat against the ground. Cross your arms across your chest, hands on opposite shoulders. Slowly curl your head, shoulders, and upper back off the floor, bringing your elbows to your thighs. Breathe out and lie back down. Repeat 10 times, or see how many you can do in 60 seconds.

- **Arm Swings and Circles (Shoulders)**
  Raise both arms in front of you so they are level to the ground. Swing them to the left, then the right. Repeat. Rest a few seconds. Then raise your arms out to your sides so they are level to the ground. Cup your hands, palm down, and make 10 medium-sized circles in the air. Do a set of 10, moving your hands forward (counterclockwise), then do 10 moving your hands backward (clockwise).

Celebrity Profile

Ivan "Pudge" Rodriguez

The Texas Rangers' Gold Glove backstop has one of the best arms of any catcher in baseball history. In 1999, he set a Major League record by throwing out more than half (53%) the base runners who tried to steal on him. A catcher who throws out one of every three base stealers is considered good!

- **Towel Pull (Shoulder)**

  Player A stands with his back to Player B, who holds out a hand towel, an old shirt, or a piece of rope. Player A reaches behind and grabs the towel. Player A then takes a step to throw and tugs the towel as if trying to throw it, like a ball. Meanwhile, Player B holds on to the towel, but does not try to yank it from Player A. Do two sets of 10, then switch positions.

On the first warm day of spring, it is tempting to head outside with a friend and immediately see who can chuck a ball the farthest and hardest. The winner—or should we say loser?—may be the first one to scream "Ow!"

Warm up your arm slowly with a few minutes of half-speed tosses, followed by a few minutes of three-quarter speed throws. "That doesn't mean lobs," says Coach John, a former college pitcher from Carmel, New York. "Snap your wrist so the throw goes on a line."

Start close in, about 10 to 15 feet (3 to 5 meters) apart. Gradually move back to a comfortable throwing distance before you let loose. "Don't grip the ball too tightly," adds John. "That could put a strain on your elbow."

At the end of a throwing workout, you need to keep your arm muscles warm. Otherwise, they might tighten up and be less flexible—and more injury prone—the next time you throw. Put on a sweatshirt or jacket. Even when it's hot out, Coach Scott covers his throwing arm from elbow to shoulder with a tube sock whose toes have been cut off.

And don't forget to stretch!

- **Elbow Rotators (Forearms)**
  Hold a light weight in each hand, palms up, straight out in front of your body. Bend your elbows slightly. Turn your wrists over, so the weights face the ground, then quickly turn your wrists back facing up. Repeat 10 times. Rest 15 seconds and repeat 10 more times.

- **Flick It (Wrists)**
  Two players stand 10 feet (3 meters) apart with their throwing-arm elbows in their mitts. Play catch, but throw with your wrist only. Follow through and put backspin on your tosses. Repeat 10 times.

Light Weights

A light weight is one that is between 1 and 4 pounds (.5 and 2 kilograms). Always start out at 1 or 2 pounds (1 kilogram). Never go over 4 pounds.

Don't have any weights? Use a can of soup, a tennis ball can filled with sand, or a plastic bag filled with marbles.

- **One Knee (Arms, shoulder, trunk)**

  Two players stand 5 to 10 feet (2 to 3 meters) apart. Each player gets down on his throwing (rear) knee and steps forward with his stride foot. Toss the ball back and forth. Complete 10 throws in a row without missing, then move back another 5 to 10 feet and repeat.

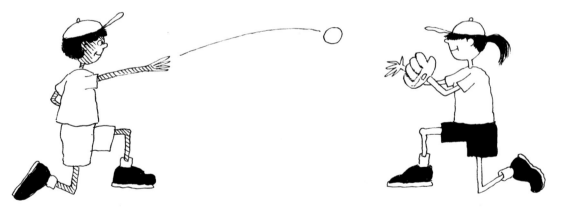

- **Leg Exercises**

  Put both feet together and jump up a few steps to a landing. Or jump in place, jog, bicycle, walk up stairs two at a time, or do wind sprints. All give your legs a good workout.

  For more leg exercises see chapter three, "Running."

Throwing Tip #2   Don't Overdo It

Caution: Pick and choose only a few of the throwing drills described here each time you work out. When your arm gets tired, rest. Even a "rifle" for an arm needs to reload after firing its "bullets."

Resting your arm is not only smart, it's the law! To make sure kids don't throw out their arms, <u>The Little League Rulebook</u> limits pitchers to a maximum of six innings a week.

Throwing Drills

Get your on-field skills in shape with these practice drills.

For One Player

- **Target Practice**
  The strike zone may look as big—or small—as a postage stamp when you're on the mound with the bases loaded and a 3–2 count. But get out a yardstick and you'll find that the strike zone measures a full 17 inches (43 centimeters) across (the width of the plate) and about 30 inches (76 centimeters) high (a little more or less, depending on the distance between the batter's knees and armpits). That's about the size of three notebooks opened and stacked on top of each other.

  To practice accuracy, throw at a target such as a tire hanging from a tree limb. Or make a strike zone: Tack a piece of paper or a cloth onto a tree trunk, draw a chalk outline on a brick wall, or stick a duct-tape rectangle onto the side of a garage. (*Hint*: Cover your homemade strike zone with wrapping paper and you'll hear each time you toss a strike.)

GOOD FOLLOW-THROUGH, BUT DON'T FORGET TO COCK YOUR WRIST BEHIND YOUR EAR.

Start with 20 throws from 20 feet (6 meters) away. Keep track of your balls and strikes on a progress chart (see page 76). Move back to 30 feet (9 meters), then 40 feet (12 meters), and finally 46 feet (14 meters)—the distance from the mound to the home plate in Little League. *Variation:* Divide and mark the strike zone into four equal sections.

Throwing Tip #3 Pitching Accuracy

"I don't care if a kid can throw faster than Pedro Martinez," says longtime Little League coach Jonathan of Edgemont, New York. "I want a pitcher who can put the ball over the plate. Control wins games, not speed." To improve accuracy, point your glove at the target before you throw.

For Two Players

- **Quick Catch**
  Stand 30 feet (9 meters) or so apart. Record the number of throws you can make in a minute without missing.

- **Step Back**
  Stand 20 feet (6 meters) apart. Take a step back after each successful catch. For each miss, step in. Go back no more than 90 feet (27 meters), approximately the distance from second base to home plate on a Little League field. Record how many catches you make without missing.

- **Bulls-eye**
  Stand 60 feet (18 meters) apart (the distance between the bases) or less. As you play catch, score 5 points for throws that come in at the chest; 3 points for the hips; 1 point for the arms, legs, or head. Deduct 1 point for throws away from the body, and 3 points for unreachable (wild) throws. The first player to get 50 points wins.

For Three or More Players

To do these, you'll need access to a ballfield.

- **Pinball Toss**
  Fill as many positions as you have players. One person directs the action, calling where the ball should get thrown. Take turns throwing from different positions.

- **Hit the Bases**
  Practice making the throw from each position to a different base. For example: from first to third, second to third,

shortstop to third, and so on. From each outfield position, make the throw to second base.

- Hit the Cutoff
Practice relay throws from each outfield position (LF, CF, RF) to the designated cutoff player (an infielder), who then throws to the catcher. A fourth player can be the runner on third tagging up. *Variation:* Have three or four players line up about 50 feet (15 meters) from each other. Player A tosses the ball a few feet away, chases after and picks it up, then throws to Player B, who repeats the sequence to Player C, and so on.

- Target Practice for Three—Pitcher, Catcher, Batter
Caution: Batters should wear a helmet for this drill.

  The pitcher throws 10 pitches. The catcher decides if they are balls or strikes. The batter doesn't swing at any of the pitches. Rather, the batter "tracks" (follows with his eyes) the pitch from the pitcher's hand into the catcher's mitt, then compares his opinion with the catcher. (Still no swinging!) After 10 pitches, players switch positions.

Cool Down

After a workout or series of drills, it's important to drink a glass of water and follow the general cool-down plan described in chapter one. Deep-stretch the muscles you've used most.

The Roger Clemens Workout

Few "power" pitchers—those who rely on throwing fastballs past batters—have lasted as long as Roger "the Rocket" Clemens. Even in his late thirties, a radar gun clocked Clemens's heater traveling in the high nineties (miles per hour).

The secret to Clemens's long success is his hard work, dedication, and commitment to staying in shape. During the off-season he rarely takes a day off from working out! He runs, lifts weights, and does calisthenics and agility exercises for 5 hours a day.

Here are a few highlights from the Rocket's in-season routine:

Day One (the day after pitching a game): 35 minutes of aerobic exercises, upper- and lower-body strength training, and quick-start drills.

Day Two: 25 minutes on an exercise bike, 25 minutes on a treadmill, and abdominal (stomach) exercises.

Day Three: Run 3½ miles (5.5 kilometers) in about 25 minutes, followed by more leg and abdominal exercises.

Day Four (the day before a start): 15 wind sprints.

Day Five (game day): 5 to 10 laps around the stadium ramps, arm- and shoulder-strengthening exercises, and a full-body stretch.

Chapter Three
Running

You're leading off third with one down and a 2–2 tie. The batter lofts a lazy fly to right for what will surely be an easy out. You go back to the bag to tag. The second the ball is caught you take off for home like a jackrabbit. The right fielder guns a frozen rope to the catcher . . . He sweeps his glove across the plate . . . too late! You score and put your team ahead.

Whether you're tagging up, stealing second, charging a slow roller, or locomoting down the line, baseball demands—and rewards—fleet feet. Expect to sprint, frequently, on offense and defense.

Some people are born with naturally fast-reacting muscles. You may never beat these speed demons in a 50-yard (46-meter) dash. But you can make it a race by being in shape and practicing good running technique.

Your legs, mainly the thigh and buttocks muscles, give you the explosive power you need for quick starts and short sprints. Follow these workout tips and drill exercises, and you may end up with a new nickname—in a flash.

Warm Up and Stretch

Before you begin your running workout, always do from 10 to 15 minutes of warm-ups and stretching exercises (see chapter one).

Running Workout

Do these exercises to develop strength.

- Tippy Toers

    Stand with your legs a few inches apart. Rise up on the balls of both feet. Hold for 10 seconds. Repeat 10 times.

- Stair Climbers

    While standing, put your hands on your hips and take a big step forward. Make sure your knee stays just over your toes. Then slowly lower your body. Pull it back to a standing position. Repeat 5 to 10 times and switch legs.

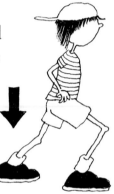

Celebrity Profile

Rickey Henderson

Rickey Henderson didn't become the all-time stolen base king on raw speed alone. He studied pitchers' pick-off moves, kept notes on catchers' throwing arms, and watched videotapes of himself stealing.

Henderson also kept himself in superb condition. In 1998, at age thirty-nine, he led the American League with sixty-six stolen bases! Almost as impressive is that he was caught just thirteen times.

- Wall Slides

  Stand with your back against a wall, hands on hips. Squat down and lower your behind into a sitting position so your feet are under your knees, as if you are in an imaginary chair. Hold for 10 seconds and build up to 30 seconds.

Running Tip # 1 Proper Form

Of course, you don't just run with your legs. The pistonlike movements of your arms help propel you forward (momentum). Run with proper form and you'll soon get to where you're going—sooner! How? Cup your hands, bend your elbows, lift your arms to your shoulders, and pump! Each arm should swing in the opposite direction of the foot moving forward.

CUP YOUR HANDS. BEND YOUR ELBOWS. LIFT YOUR ARMS. PUMP!

Quick Quiz

1. You're leading off third in foul territory. The batter smashes a one-hopper that bounces off your foot.

   a. The batter is out for hitting you with the ball.
   b. You are out for being hit by a batted ball.
   c. Neither you nor the batter is out. But the coach takes you out of the game because you have a black-and-blue mark on your foot.

   ANSWER: c. Always lead from third in foul territory. If struck by a batted ball in fair territory, you will be called out for interfering with a fair ball. How far should you lead from third? About as many steps from the bag as the third baseman.

2. You're on first. The coach flashes the sacrifice bunt signal. You get ready to dig hard to second. The batter squares around but misses the pitch.

   a. You head to second anyway, figuring why waste a good lead and all that adrenaline.
   b. You scoot back to first.
   c. Nothing happens, so you stay where you are.

   ANSWER b. Don't run on a missed bunt. You could be thrown out stealing or get picked off.

3. You're on first with one away. The batter hits a looping liner that the left fielder has to charge.

   a. You figure he'll never catch it, so you take off at a full gallop determined to score the go-ahead run.
   b. You stay on the base, ready to tag up.
   c. You go halfway to second to see what happens.

   ANSWER: c. It's not a tag situation (answer b), and you don't want to risk being doubled up (answer a). Go halfway to the next base on balls hit to the outfield that might get caught in the air.

Running Tip # 2 It's Mental

Fast runners have speedy brains, too! Make it a habit to always know the count and number of outs.

And always note what's happening on the field. Are the outfielders shallow or deep? Who has a rifle for an arm? Who doesn't? Who's got a limp noodle you can challenge on the base paths? Who doesn't? Is the third baseman playing deep enough for you to leg out a surprise bunt?

Watch the coach for signals so there's no hesitation or second-guessing on your part.

- Ceiling Grabs
  While standing, flex your knees, drop your arms behind you, jump up, raise your arms in front, and try to touch the ceiling. Repeat 5 to 10 times.

- High Steppers
  While standing, put your hands on your hips. Run in place for 30 seconds, making sure to raise your knees high.

Do these exercises to develop agility and stamina.

- Hoop Hops
  Stagger six or more hula hoops (left, right) on the ground (or draw large circles) and run through them forward then backward. Time yourself and keep track on a progress chart.

- Mitt Jumps
  Place your mitt on the ground. Put your feet together and jump sideways over the mitt 10 times without stopping. Repeat with forward and backward jumps.

Running Drills

Get your on-field skills in shape with these practice drills.

- Shuttle Run (One or more players)
  Line up three (or more) balls a foot apart. Stand 15 to 20 feet (5 to 6 meters) from the balls. On "go" run in, pick up one ball, and backpedal to the starting line. Continue for two (or more) balls. Time yourself. See how you improve. Compare your time with a friend. *Variation:* Two players compete at the same time. Whoever finishes first wins.

- Touchdown! (Two or more players)
  One person is the "quarterback" (QB). As each "receiver" jogs by, he flips a ball to the QB. Then the receiver sprints

Running Tip # 3   Running to First

You top one too short and need to hustle to beat the throw. Make the first step out of the batter's box with your back foot. Follow with short, quick steps, gradually lengthening your stride. Glance at the fielder to make sure the play is on, then race to the base. Run past first base at full speed. (Lean forward, as if crossing a finish line.) If possible, your left foot should touch the outside corner of the bag. Continue straight down the foul line,

looking over your right shoulder for instructions from the coach, or for a wild throw. Slow down with short, choppy steps.

Do NOT turn left (toward second base) after you pass first base. That puts you in fair territory, which means you can be tagged out. To help you get in the habit of running past first, place a cone or marker 10 feet (3 meters) beyond the bag during practice runs.

downfield as if going out for a forward pass. The QB yells left, right, or straight (the direction the ball will be thrown) and lobs the ball toward the receiver, who makes the catch on a fly and jogs back. Players take turns "passing" and "receiving." *Variation:* Use tennis balls and no mitt for a good "soft hands" fielding drill.

Fun Runs

Practicing real-game situations by yourself or with a friend will help you develop anticipation, or "good instincts," which translates into faster reactions, better reflexes, and improved quickness. Your mind and body will seem to know what to do even before you make the play.

- **Pretend At Bats**
  Start at the plate with a bat. Take a swing and pretend to hit the ball. Drop your bat (carefully!) and run toward first. Your friend directs the action, yelling out what happens next on your pretend at bat. For example: "Grounder to short!" means dig hard and run past the bag. "Single to left" means take the turn at first. "In the gap" means go for a double.

- **Pretend on the Base Paths**
  Start at first base. Practice taking a lead (if your league allows it). Go to second on a sacrifice bunt. Score from second on a hit. Tag up on a fly ball. Exercise your imagination and come up with other scenarios.

- **On Your Mark, Get Set, Go-go-go!**
  How fast are you running from home to first? Home to second? First to third? Tagging up from third? Get a stop-

watch, a friend, and a ballfield and time yourself! Keep track on a progress chart. (Rest between each run and do them on separate days.)

- Off to the Races
  One player starts at home plate. The other starts on second base. On "go," race to see who crosses home/second first.

Cool Down

After a workout, it's important to cool down and stretch out those freshly exercised muscles. Drink a glass of water and follow the general cool-down plan described in chapter one. Deep-stretch the muscles you used most.

You lace one into the gap in right and hightail it out of the box, thinking two-bagger. When stretching a single into a double, aim for the inside corner of first base with your left foot (but don't break your stride).

To help you make the turn, or "round the bag," you'll need to make an arc, or semicircle approach to first base. At about 12 feet (4 meters) from the bag, curve out to the right, then back left. By "cutting the corner" you won't have to shift direction or lose momentum.

To practice, place one cone or marker about 12 feet (4 meters) in front of the base and 3 feet (1 meter) to the right. Place a second cone or marker 15 feet (5 meters) past first base and 6 feet (2 meters) in from the baseline. Stay on the left side of the second cone.

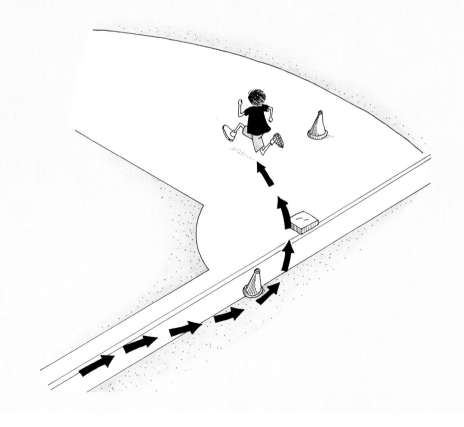

Chapter Four
Hitting for Average

THWACK!

You're up with two down, a runner on second, and a tie score. The count is one ball, two strikes—a pitcher's count—so you choke up an inch. The next pitch is a little high and inside, but you have to protect the plate and . . . WHAP! You belt the ball a country mile . . . FOUL! Back to the batter's box you trot. You foul off two more close pitches, patiently waiting for . . . here it comes . . . a low one on the outside part of the plate. You swing easy, level, and the ball zips through the hole between first and second. The runner scores!

Hitting is a cinch, right? Just plant your back foot, bend your knees, hold your hands away, elbows up, wrists cocked, chin tucked, eyes on the ball, front shoulder down, stride-foot parallel . . . okay, okay. Hitting a baseball is actually just about the hardest thing to do in ALL sports. The best batters fail two out of three times!

What does it take to be a good hitter? Strong arms, quick wrists, powerful legs, sharp eyes, and, of course, a good head on your shoulders. Even then, you won't hit a lick if all these body parts—think of them as members of your personal "swat" team—are out of sync.

Warm Up and Stretch

Before you begin working out and doing drills, always do from 10 to 15 minutes of warm-ups and stretching exercises (see chapter one).

How to Hit .000

To see how your body parts work together, take a few of the following intentional mis-swings. After each one, note what body part has been left out and how it impacted your swing. Then you'll be able to recognize them—and work on overcoming bad habits.

1. Put both feet together. Swing without taking a step. Result?

2. Put both feet too far apart (beyond shoulder width). Swing without taking a step. Result?

3. Assume your regular balanced stance with feet about shoulders' width apart. Swing without taking a step. Result?

4. Assume your regular stance. Take a too-big step on your front foot; step forward on your back foot as you follow through. Result?

5. Take your usual swing. Stiffen your stride leg. Result?

6. Swing with your lead arm only. (Left arm if you bat right-handed.) Result?

7. Swing with your top arm only. (Right arm if you bat right-handed.) Result?

8. Squeeze the bat tight. Result?

9. Swing without "breaking" your wrists. Result?

10. Let your gaze drift upward as you swing. Result?

ANSWERS: 1. lower body; off balance; 2. legs; no power; 3. hips; no power; 4. feet; off balance—loss of control; 5. knee; off balance—loss of power; 6. arm; loss of control; 7. arm; loss of control; 8. hands; slows the swing (A loose grip gives you more flexibility and hand speed. Your muscles naturally grip the bat tighter on contact.); 9. wrists; loss of power and control; 10. eyes; loss of control

Hitting for Average Workout

Exercises like jumping jacks, push-ups, and sit-ups will strengthen your shoulders, chest, back, and trunk. These muscle groups support and stabilize your body's two main power centers: your arms and midsection. These other exercises will increase your hand strength, balance, and ability to "see" the ball at bat. You can do them anytime, anywhere.

- **Squeeze Balls**
  Squeezing a soft rubber ball or tennis ball will strengthen your wrists and forearms. This was a favorite exercise of baseball great, Ted Williams.

Hitting Tip # 1   See the Ball

It takes less than half a second for a Major League fastball to travel from the mound to the plate. In the blink of an eye, hitters must decide if they're going to swing—and also take that swing.

Good hitters watch the ball right out of the pitcher's hand. But staring at the pitcher throughout his windup will only tire your eyes, causing you to lose concentration when you need it most.

Coaches at the Frozen Ropes Training Center based in Chester, New York, train batters to focus their eyes two ways. During the windup, batters <u>soft focus</u> (like during a daydream) on the pitcher's hat. Then, just as the pitcher is about to throw the ball, batters shift to a <u>fine focus</u> (like staring) at the pitcher's release point.

Opening your stance slightly should make it easier to focus both eyes on the pitcher. But as you swing, remember to close your stance and stride toward the pitcher.

- **One Arm**

  Your bottom-hand (lead) arm controls your swing. You can get it into shape almost anytime—and without a bat. Practice slow, level swings with just the lead arm. *Variation:* With your lead arm, grab a bat about a third of the way up the handle and take some cuts.

- **Hop to It**

  This exercise will help you stay balanced during—and after—your swing. Assume your usual stance, but without a bat in your hand. Get into Swing Position #2 (see page 45): bat back, weight on your back foot, stride foot off the ground, knee pointing backward. Raise your stride-foot knee high, then lower it, without touching the ground. Repeat 3 times, then step forward and swing (making sure you keep your back foot on the ground).

- **See the Tree, See the Leaf**

  This vision drill will help a hitter learn how to pick up the ball out of a pitcher's hand. (Shift from a soft to a fine focus.) Relax your eyes and gaze at a tree in the near distance. Hold for a few seconds (approximately the amount of time it takes a pitcher to wind up). Then quickly shift focus to a single leaf on a branch. Keep your head still, moving your eyes only. *Variation:* Stand in the batter's box and face a pitcher. Soft focus on the pitcher's cap as he goes into the windup, then shift to a fine focus at the release point of the throw. (*Note:* The pitcher only pretends to throw the ball!)

There are plenty of <u>wrong</u> ways to hit, but there's no one right way. "Hitting is more art than science, with ample room for personal style," says Coach Scott. Some .300 batters crouch and crowd the plate. Others stand tall and deep in the box. Some hold their hands high. Others hold their hands low.

When you step into the batter's box, be comfortable, be confident, and be yourself. But follow these five basic steps:

1. Stand evenly balanced on the balls of your feet, knees flexed. Relax; don't squeeze the bat too tight.

2. When the pitch is released, shift your weight to your back foot and roll your shoulders and hips away from the pitcher.

3. Step forward with your stride (front) foot and shift your weight back toward the pitcher. Keep the big toe of your back foot on the ground.

4. Twist (uncoil) your hips until your belt buckle faces the pitcher, bringing your arms over, then in front of the plate. Your lead-arm's hand should be facing palm down. This is the ideal "hitting position."

5. Strike the ball, but continue swinging. Roll over your wrists with your bottom hand providing the power. Finish the swing with your bottom hand leading. Reach your hands toward the pitcher, then quickly draw your forearms across your body and bring your wrists up over your shoulder.

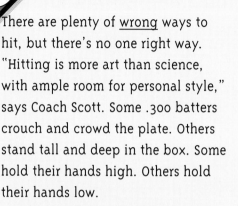

...AND DON'T FORGET RULE #1: WATCH THE **BALL** HIT THE **BAT !**

Hitting for Average Drills

Get your on-field skills in shape with these practice drills.

For One or More Players

These exercises will help you develop proper swing technique.

- Study Your Swing #1
  Without a bat, watch yourself swing in a mirror. Check your stance and the position of your hands and hips.

- Study Your Swing #2
  With a bat, videotape your swing. Watch the replay in slow-mo. Pretend you're a TV sports announcer. Analyze your swing "for the viewers at home."

- Slide 'n' Strike
  To prevent overstriding, place a brick about 4 to 6 inches (10 to 15 centimeters) in front of your stride foot. Raise your foot just off the ground, then slide it until the side of your foot touches the brick. Try not to move the brick. If your toe hits the brick, you're opening up your hips too soon, or stepping inside ("in the bucket").

- Squash the Bug
  During a typical swing, your back heel naturally rises and spins out as your hips turn. But if the toes on your back foot come off the ground, the force of the swing will cause you to step forward. You'll lose control of your swing and might fall! Practice swinging (with or without a bat) and pretend you're squashing bugs with the toes of your back foot.

- **Blast Off!**

  Tie a string around a plastic ball. Hang it from a pipe in a basement, a rafter in a garage, or a tree limb so it dangles about waist high. Invent game situations and pitch counts. Call the pitch and swing away! (Keep your eye on the ball and follow through.) *Variation:* Use a "ball" made from a pair of socks.

- **Tee Ball**

  If the stand that the ball sits on can be moved, place it into the ideal hitting zone: a few inches in front of—not in the middle of—the plate. (Hitting a ball in front of the plate allows you to extend your arms for full power on contact). Practice hitting to all fields. Move the stand a few inches further from the plate for inside pitches and closer to the plate for outside pitches. Adjust the height for high and

Hitting Tip # 3
Swing Down on the Ball

When a pro loosens up in the on-deck circle, he'll often swing with a slightly downward motion. Why? When the bat contacts the incoming ball at this angle, the ball flies off with upward spin, which makes it climb.

Hitting Tip # 4
Take a Pitch

When up against a new pitcher, let the first throw go by, even if it's a fat one right down Broadway. Taking a pitch helps a batter gauge the pitcher's speed and become familiar with his delivery.

low pitches. *Variation I:* Create game situations. What's the count? Where are the base runners? How many outs? Take a swing! *Variation II:* Get a friend to field your hits. Switch places after 10 swings or 3 outs.

- Strike Zone (Pitcher, Catcher, Batter)
  Caution: Batters should wear a helmet for this drill.

"A good hitter will follow a pitch right into the catcher's glove," says Coach Vic of Yonkers, New York.

The pitcher throws 10 pitches. The batter doesn't swing at any of the pitches. Rather, the batter "tracks" (follows with his eyes) the pitch from the pitcher's hand into the catcher's mitt. The batter decides if it is a ball or a strike, then compares his opinion with the catcher. (Still no swinging!) After 10 pitches, players switch positions.

For Two Players

These exercises will help develop better hand-eye coordination.

- **Soft Toss**
  The batter takes a regular stance. The pitcher kneels about 10 feet (3 meters) away from the plate on a 45-degree angle. The pitcher underhand-tosses a soft, spongy ball about waist high and slightly in front of the plate. The batter tries to drive the ball straight up the middle. *Variation:* The batter uses a 30-inch (76-centimeter) broomstick.

- **Small Ball**
  The pitcher kneels 3 feet (1 meter) away from the plate on a 45-degree angle and tosses plastic golf balls to the batter. *Variations:* Toss marshmallows, corks, or small beanbags.

- **Hit the Birdie**
  The pitcher stands 10 to 15 feet (3 to 5 meters) in front of the batter and pitches badminton birdies, overhand.

Cool Down

After a workout, it's important to cool down and stretch out those freshly exercised muscles. Drink a glass of water and follow the general cool-down plan described in chapter one. Deep-stretch the muscles you've been using most.

Chapter Five
Hitting with Power

The bases are loaded, with two out in the bottom of the ninth. Your team is down by 3. But you're pumped 'cause the count is 3 and 1—a hitter's count—and you tagged this mope for a double back in the fifth.

The pitcher rears back and brings some heat down the pike . . . THWACK! It's going back, back, back . . . kiss it good-bye! The team goes wild. The crowd goes wild. You're a grand-slam hero!

Few thrills in baseball, or any sport, compare to smacking a game-winning homer in the bottom of the ninth. In the last chapter you learned how to groove a smooth, level swing. This chapter will help you add pop to your stroke.

Warm Up and Stretch

Have you ever seen a pro ballplayer step into the batter's box without limbering up and taking a few practice cuts in the on-deck circle first? Of course not! They wouldn't risk an injury—and neither should you (even if you don't make their big bucks—yet).

Swinging a bat requires quick, explosive movements that can rupture cold muscles. Warm up and stretch before you try the following "bat-tercises" (exercises with a bat).

Hitting with Power Workout

Caution: When your arms begin to tire, wind down your workout. Fatigue can lead to poorly executed practice swings, which may do more harm than good.

- **Bat Circles (Shoulder)**
  Hold the bat in one hand at the knob and straight out to your side. Swing it over your head in large, clockwise circles 5 times. Rest for 5 seconds, then swing the bat in the other direction 5 times. Repeat both exercises with the other arm.

- **Bat Raises (Wrist, forearm)**
  Hold the bat in one hand just below the knob and facing straight down. Cock your wrist to raise the bat until the tip is level with your waist. Repeat 5 times, then switch hands.

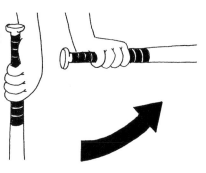

- **Wrist Wriggles (Wrists, forearms)**
  Get into Swing Position #3 (see page 45) as if you're about to hit the ball. Roll your *wrists only* forward and back 10 times. Repeat, increasing the arc so your forearms, elbows, and hands swing from shoulder to shoulder.

- **Bat Lifts #1 (Upper arm)**
  Hold the bat in one hand at the knob and facing straight down. Extend your arm in front of you and slowly lift the bat until it is even with your waist, then slowly lower the bat. Repeat 5 times, then switch arms.

- Bat Lifts #2 (Upper arm)
  Hold the bat in one hand at the knob and straight out in front of you, even with your waist. Bend your elbow and lift the bat up. Repeat 5 times, then switch arms.

- Bat Twists #1 (Trunk, hips, arms)
  Hold the bat in front of you with one hand on each end, chest high, parallel to the ground. Turn at the waist as far as you can to the right and hold for a count of 3. Turn at the waist as far as you can to the left for a count of 3. Repeat 3 times.

  RIGHT TURN

- Bat Twists #2 (Trunk, hips, arms)
  Put the bat behind your back and hold in the crook of your elbows. Slowly turn to the right and hold for 15 seconds. Slowly turn to the left and hold for 15 seconds.

  RIGHT TURN

Hitting Tip # 1
Use a Batting Cage

Some batting cages can be rented on an hourly basis. Go with a few friends and split the cost.

Hitting Tip # 2   Stick Selection

You want to bash the ball into smithereens. Should you switch to a bigger bat? Swing from the heels with all your might? Only if you want to increase your strike outs! To hit with power, you need to swing <u>faster</u>—not harder. "It's better to use a light bat that you can control," says Coach John. Players who swing a too-heavy or too-long bat tend to drop their back shoulder and uppercut rather than swing level.

You should be able to hold your bat in front of you for 25 seconds in each hand. Every ounce counts. Using a light bat with a thin handle may increase your swing speed.

To increase the speed of your swing, or <u>bat speed</u>, you need to strengthen your upper body, especially your hands, wrists, and forearms. Well-conditioned thigh and stomach muscles will also help you generate more power. These large muscles pull the hips around and the upper body into the ideal hitting position (see chapter four, p. 45).

HOLD... 23... 24... 25. **WHEW!**

- **Bat Strides (Hips)**

  Hold the bat behind your back in the crook of your elbows. Pretend you're facing the plate. Step sideways on your front leg (toward the pitcher's mound) about 6 inches (15 centimeters) and quickly turn (thrust) your back hip toward the mound. Let your back foot spin around, but keep the toes on the ground. Repeat 5 times.

- **Bat Hangs (Stomach, back)**

  Put the bat behind your neck and across your shoulders. Let your wrists hang limply over the ends. Flex your knees, touch your chin to your chest, and slowly bend at the waist. Hold for 30 seconds.

- **Bat Battle (Upper body)**

  This is a two-person exercise. The batter gets into Swing Position #3 with the bat across the middle of the plate. The nonbatter stands facing the batter and pushes against the barrel of the bat as the batter tries to complete the swing. Push for 10 seconds. Rest for 10 seconds. Repeat 3 times.

- **Hit the Tire (Upper body)**

  Hang a tire or heavy bag from a tree limb so its middle is even with your waist. Mark an X on the side of the tire and pretend it's the ball coming at you. Swing the bat at the tire forcefully, as if trying to slice it in half. Maintain your balance. Steady the tire after each swing. Swing 5 times, rest, and repeat.

Celebrity Profile

Hank Aaron

You don't have to be as huge as Mark McGwire, 6 feet 5 inches and 240 pounds (2 plus meters and 109 kilograms), to jack the ball out of the park. All-time home-run king Hank Aaron stood just 6 feet tall and weighed 180 pounds (2 meters and 82 kilograms). His secret: He had incredibly strong and quick wrists.

- **Donut/No Donut (Bat-speed drill)**
  Place a *donut* (a circular, donut-shaped weight) over the knob of the bat and slide it down the handle until it fits snugly around the barrel. Take 10 full cuts. Make sure your final swing is as fast, strong, and level as the first. Remove the donut, rest. Take 10 more swings. Notice how light the bat feels. *Variation:* Combine with the *Blast Off!* (hanging ball) drill (see page 47).

Hitting With Power Drills

Get your on-field skills in shape with these practice drills.

- One-Arm Soft Toss (Two-player drill)
  The batter uses a smaller-than-usual bat, such as a Tee-ball bat, which he holds in his bottom hand (the left hand for a right-handed batter). The nonbatter kneels in front of the plate, as in *Soft Toss* (see page 49), and underhand-throws tennis balls to different parts of the strike zone. After 10 swings with the bat in each arm, players switch positions.

- Batting Cage
  There is no substitute for hitting against live pitching—even if it's from a machine. For each round of pitches, give yourself a specific goal, such as pulling the ball. Or concentrate on one part of your swing, such as following through. To help you work on your timing, alternate between cages with different speeds.

Cool Down

After a workout, it's important to cool down and stretch out those freshly exercised muscles. Drink a glass of water and follow the general cool-down plan described in chapter one. Deep-stretch the muscles you've just been using most.

Chapter Six
Fielding

You're playing second with runners on first and third, one away. The batter whacks a wicked grass-burner up the middle for a sure RBI single. Wait! You dive to your right, snag the ball, and—what a play! —flip it from your glove to the shortstop who toes second for one. She leaps high over the hard-sliding runner and pegs the ball to first. The throw's low, but the first baseman picks it out of the dirt for two. A bang-bang 4–6–3 double play and the inning is over!

Half of the game of baseball is defense. If you're slick with a mitt, you'll always have a place in the lineup.

But just because there are only three basic plays— grounders, line drives, and fly balls—doesn't mean fielding is easy! A good "glove man" (or woman!) needs quick hands, quick feet, and quick wits. As soon as a ball leaves the bat, fielders need to make one of many special moves to get to the ball as quickly as possible:

- Backpedal for short pops
- Charge or rush in on slow grounders
- Glide side-to-side to reach hard grounders
- Use a *crossover step* to turn in the direction of balls hit farther away
- Use a *drop step* to track down long fly balls (See the *Turn and Go!* drill, page 66)

After lots of practice, you'll find yourself making these moves instinctively.

Warm Up and Stretch

Before you begin your fielding workout, always do from 10 to 15 minutes of warm-ups and stretching exercises (see chapter one).

Fielding Workout

Out in the field, expect to bend low, reach high, and dart and dive in all directions. "And be ready to run every time the ball is hit," says Coach Vic, "even if the ball is not hit to you. If you're not in motion, you're not doing your job. You should be covering a base or backing up a player who is." These exercises will increase your agility and stamina.

- Trunk Twists
  Hold your glove between your hands. Swing your arms as far as you can to the left. Hold for 3 seconds. Swing your arms to your right. Hold for 3 seconds. Repeat.

- Bat Jumps
  Put a bat on the ground. Keep your feet together and hop over it sideways, then back again, for 30 seconds without stopping. Make sure to draw your knees up high.

- One Leg
  Stand on one leg keeping your heel flat on the ground. Bend your knee, lean forward, then push off the ground with your fingertips. Rise to a standing position, still on one leg. Repeat 10 times, then switch legs.

- Pick-a-Penny

  Face off against a friend. Place nine pennies or pebbles on the ground or floor. Get into the fielding ready position (hands on knees, bent slightly, weight resting on the balls of your feet). On "Go!" reach down with your throwing hand and pick up one penny. Stand and place it in a cup on a side table next to you. The first to pick up five pennies wins.

- Speedy Shuffle

  While standing, bend your knees and raise both arms out in front of you. Shuffle-step quickly to the left for 10 yards (9 meters), then back. (Don't cross your feet as you move.)

- Ladder Run

  Draw a long ladder on a flat area. Run forward and backward, stepping between each "rung" with each foot.

- Coin Catch

  Get into the fielding ready position. Flip a coin into the air with your throwing hand and catch it in your bare glove hand, palm up. Repeat 10 times. Record the number of "outs" and "errors." Repeat the exercise and catch the coin palm down. (*Hint:* Larger coins are easier than smaller coins.)

Fielding Drills

Get your on-field skills in shape with these practice drills.

For One Player

- **Wall Ball**

  Mark an X on a wall about 2 feet (.6 meter) from the ground. Throw a ball that's soft (such as a rubber ball or a tennis ball) at the target, catching the ball on one bounce. How many plays can you make without an error?

  For harder grounders, move the target lower down on the wall, or move farther back from the wall. For a "soft hands" drill, do not use a mitt and move closer to the wall. Count the number of catches you make in 30 seconds.

- **Self-Toss**

  Throw high flies and chase them down! To help simulate a real game situation, run at half speed, toss the ball high and about 10 feet (9 meters) in front of you. Then go at full tilt to catch it.

For Two Players

- **Lean and Mean**

  Lay a bat on the ground in front of you. Place your feet right behind the bat. Move your throwing foot back a few inches. Have your partner roll slow grounders, which you field *in front of* the bat.

Willie Mays Makes "The Catch"

One of the niftiest fielding gems in baseball history happened during Game One of the 1954 World Series and is known simply as "The Catch." With a 2–2 tie in the eighth and two players on, the Cleveland Indians slugger Vic Wertz sent a towering drive to straightaway center field. At the crack of the bat, twenty-three-year-old New York Giants center fielder Willie Mays turned his back to the plate and sprinted to the deepest part of the park, catching up with the ball some 440 feet (134 meters) away. Even more amazing was his immediate and on-line throw back to the infield, which prevented the runners from scoring. The Giants won the game in extra innings, and swept the series four games to none.

In addition to his many batting and running achievements, All-Century Team member Willie Mays won the Gold Glove award twelve years in a row (1957–1968).

Fielding Tip # 1   Stay Low on Grounders

Catch ground balls with your hands in front of your body. Keep your head down and bend your knees. Your throwing hand covers the ball as it rolls into your mitt.

"Derek Jeter is one of the best at it," says Coach Jonathan. "I tell the kids on my team to videotape him fielding routine grounders, then study it in slow-mo."

• Soft Hands

Field grounders without a mitt. Use soft baseballs or tennis balls. Try to catch the ball in front of your feet, and draw the ball toward your body as you scoop it up. *Variations:* Wear a mitten or oven mitt on your glove hand. To practice fielding grounders with both hands, tie a thin rope about 1-foot (.3-meter) long around your wrists.

Outfield Pop (fly) Quiz

1. You're playing right field. Runners are on first and second with no outs. The batter singles to left. You:

   a. Run across the field to back up the left fielder.
   b. Stay where you are, daydreaming about the kind of topping you want on the postgame pizza.
   c. Get in position to back up a possible throw to second base.

2. You're playing left field. There's a runner on second with one away. The batter drops a bunt down the third base line. You:

   a. Run in to cover third.
   b. Yell encouragement to your teammates.
   c. Back up the third baseman's throw to the shortstop, who is covering third on the play.

3. You're playing center field. The runner on first is stealing! You:

   a. Do nothing because the infield is not your department.
   b. Don't notice what's happening because you're thinking about the next inning when you're due up at second.
   c. Run in just in case the throw from the catcher is wild.

[All answers c.]

- **Very Short Hops**
  Kneel 15 feet (5 meters) apart from each other and throw one-hop grounders to each other. Catch 10 in a row, then move farther apart.

Fielding Tip # 2
Soft Hands

No matter how sharply a ground ball is hit, try to catch it "soft." Draw the ball toward your body as you scoop it up. (Think of the ball as a baby bird that should be handled with care.)

- **Turn and Go! (Drop-step drill)**
Assume the fielder-ready position. Your partner faces you from 15 feet (5 meters) away. On the command "left" or "right," turn your body and take a step back in the direction the ball is going. Then your partner throws a fly ball in that direction, which you chase down. When possible, circle behind the ball in an arcing pattern so that you're moving back toward the infield as you catch it. That gets you in the best position to throw with forward momentum.

Field Ready   **Turn**

- Hot Potato
  Note: This drill trains infielders to get the ball out of their glove, and throw, quickly.

  Stand about 30 feet (9 meters) apart (halfway between the bases on a Little League field). See how many throws you can make in 30 seconds. Or play that whoever has the ball when 30 seconds is up loses.

- Hot Corner
  Note: This drill helps develop fast reflexes.

  Stand with your back to your partner. When your partner says "Go," turn around and try to catch the tennis ball or soft baseball your partner throws at you.

- Good Ol' Catch
  Take turns throwing slow rollers, short hops, ground balls left and right, pops, and line drives. *Variations:* Create game situations or do your own play-by-play!

For Three or More Players

- Bucket O' Balls
  One person whacks tennis balls with a tennis racket. (It's easier to handle than a bat.) One or more players take turns calling for the ball. Score 3 points for flies, 2 for hard grounders, 1 for easy grounders. Gloves optional.

- Play at the Plate
  One player stands near the pitcher's mound and throws a fly ball to an outfielder. The outfielder throws the ball to the infield cutoff player. The cutoff player throws to the catcher. The catcher tosses the ball back to the thrower/

Fielding Tip #3   Outfield Alert

Outfielders' muscles can tighten up, especially when the only flies they've seen all day are the winged kind! Jog in place, do a few jumping jacks, and stretch between batters. Keep your arm warm between innings by tossing a ball around with a teammate.

Out in the field, keep your head in the game by mentally recording the ball–strike count. Or pretend you're on the mound. What would you throw?

Before each pitch, fielders need to "know the situation," says Coach Vic. "How many outs are there?" Coach Jonathan suggests that you ask yourself, "What will I do if the ball comes my way."

batter. Give 1 point for each successful catch, throw, and relay throw. Players rotate positions after 5 plays. *Variation:* One person hits "fungoes" (self-tossed pitches) and doubles as the catcher.

- Pepper

A batter stands about 10 feet (3 meters) from a few fielders. One fielder underhand-tosses a ball to the batter, who taps it back with a short, downward half-swing. Whoever fields the ball tosses it back, quickly. After 5 to 10 swings, switch positions.

This classic fielding warm-up exercise gets its name because it is fast moving (peppy), and the batter peppers (sprays) the ball in different directions.

Fielding Tip # 4
Mitt Size Matters

Fielders catch balls, not mitts. Hall-of-Fame second baseman "Little" Joe Morgan won five Gold Glove awards with a mitt that didn't seem big enough to catch a pea.

Morgan preferred a small mitt to a larger one because it was easier to handle. He could move it into position quicker and get the ball out faster. A ball can roll around inside the pocket of a too-large mitt.

Cool Down

After a workout, it's important to cool down and stretch out those freshly exercised muscles. Drink a glass of water and follow the general cool-down plan described in chapter one. Deep-stretch the muscles you've been using most.

Chapter Seven
Baseball Games

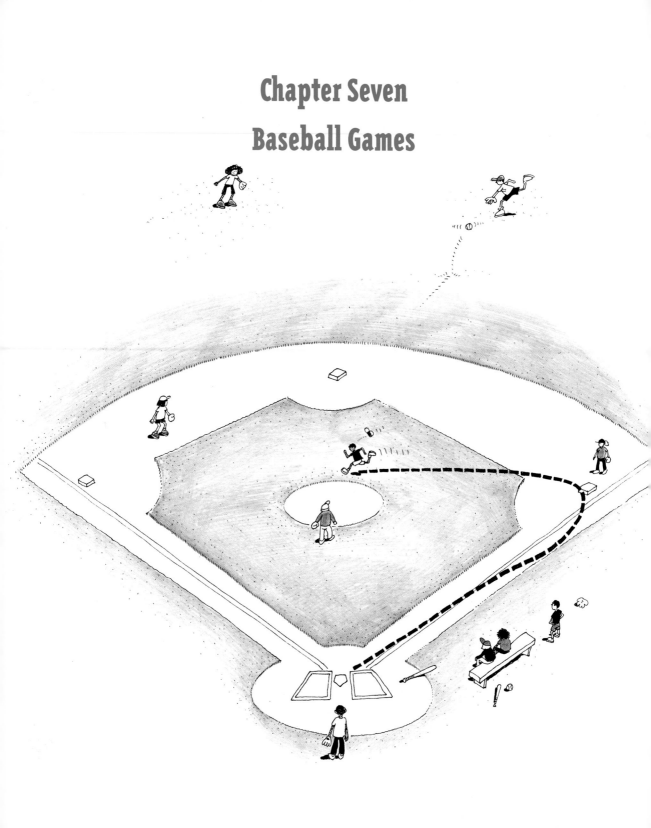

You don't need nine on a side or a formal ballfield to get in a workout—and have fun—playing these baseball-based games. But always start off with a warm up and stretch and end with a cool down.

One Bounce

What you need: A tennis ball or rubber ball, a bat or broom-stick, five or more players

What you do: The batter bounces the ball on home plate and swats it with the bat. The number of bases and fields that are considered in fair territory depends on the number of players. (For instance, if there are only a few fielders, any ball hit to the right of second base can be an automatic out or a foul ball.) Play that two or three fouls is an out, or that a batted ball caught on one bounce is an out. *Variations:* The batter punches a rubber ball or throws a tennis ball.

One Cat

What you need: A bat, a ball, two bases (home and first), and three or more players

What you do: One fielder pitches the ball. On a fair hit, the batter has to run to the one base and back home without get-ting tagged out. Players rotate positions after the batter makes three outs.

Triangle Ball

What you need: A bat, a ball, three bases (home, first, and third), and three or more players

What you do: Play is similar to One Cat. On a fair hit, the batter has to run to first, then across the infield area to third base, then back home without getting out.

Double or Nothing

What you need: A bat, a ball, four bases, and four or more players on each side

What you do: Play is similar to regular baseball, but each batter must make it to second base (or farther) or it is an out.

Three Flies Up/500 Points/Hit the Bat

What you need: A bat, a ball, three or more players, and an open area

What you do: A batter self-tosses and hits the ball (fungoes). The first fielder to catch three balls in the air (or six grounders) is up next. Or fielders can score points for each clean play, depending on the difficulty. (For example: 100 points for a fly ball; 50 points for a grounder. You can award bonus points for spectacular catches or deduct points for muffed plays.) The first fielder to reach 500 points bats.

After each hit, the batter lays the bat on the ground horizontally. If the fielder's throw back to the batter strikes the bat, the fielder earns additional points or automatically gets to bat.

Bang Ball

What you need: A windowless wall, a rubber ball or tennis ball, and three or more players

What you do: One player (the batter) bangs (throws) the ball against the wall and tries to get it past two (or more) fielders. Mark zones and score each at bat as an out, single, double, triple, or home run, depending on where the ball ends up. Play with "invisible" runners and keep score. (Invisible runners stay on base after a hit. They advance one base if the next batter hits a single, two bases for a double, etc.) Balls caught on a fly, or grounders caught in front of the single zone, are outs. After three outs, players rotate positions.

One Swing Heroes

Anybody who has ever swung a baseball bat has probably fantasized about hitting a home run in the bottom of the ninth inning to lead the team to World Series victory. But it's happened only twice in a hundred years of World Series.

1960: Bill Mazerowski's lead-off shot in the bottom of the ninth inning in Game 7 broke a 9–9 tie that boosted the Pittsburgh Pirates over the New York Yankees.

1993: Toronto Blue Jay slugger Joe Carter (right) blasted a three-run shot out of the park for a come-from-behind victory over the Philadelphia Phillies.

The Sound of a Home Run

Some of the sweetest words a batter can hear are: "Four-bagger," "dinger," "circuit clout," "tater," "long ball," "moon shot," "round-tripper," "he parked one," "what a poke," "swat," "it's outtahere," "going yard," "going deep," "he's taking the pitcher downtown," "the gopher has been fed," "kiss it good-bye!"

Can you think of other ways to say "home run?"

Home Run Derby

What you need: A bat; a ball; a narrow, flat area (such as a quiet street); and two or more players

What you do: One player self-tosses and hits the ball. If it goes past the agreed-upon "home run" line on a fly it is a run. Any other hit is an out. After three outs, switch sides. *Variations:*

1. Play with markers for a single, double, and triple and use invisible runners.

2. Have a member of your team or the opposing team pitch the ball.

3. Balls caught on a fly or grounders caught in front of the single zone are outs.

Pickle (When you're in a rundown)

What you need: Two bases, one ball, two fielders, one runner

What you do: The runner stands between the bases and tries to avoid being tagged by the fielders, who toss the ball back and forth. Whoever tags the runner gets to be in the middle. The runner who makes it safely to either base gets to go again.

Hot Box

Similar to Pickle, but with two or three runners.

Running Bases

What you need: Two bases, two fielders, one ball, two or more runners

What you do: The runners stand on one of the bases while the fielders toss the ball back and forth. Runners try to beat the throws and steal the other base without being tagged out. (Award one point for each successful steal. Allow three "caught stealing" for each runner.) Runners can run as a group, individually, or in pairs.

Skills 'n' Drills Progress Chart

Photocopy this chart and keep track of how well you do each time you try the following skill-building drills. See how you improve over time.

Player _____ Date _____

Chapter Two: Throwing

Quick catch   no. of throws in 60 seconds   _____
Step back   no. of throws without missing _____
Target practice for one
    20 throws at 20 ft. (6 meters):   balls _____ strikes _____
               at 30 ft. (9 meters):   balls _____ strikes _____
               at 40 ft. (12 meters): balls _____ strikes _____
               at 46 ft. (14 meters): balls _____ strikes _____

Chapter Three: Running

Home to first   time _____
Home to second   time _____
Home to third   time _____
Third to home (tag up)   time _____
First to third   time _____
Second to home   time _____

Chapter Four: Hitting

Batting cage   balls pitched:
                            hits _____ fouls _____ misses _____

Chapter Six: Fielding

Speedy shuffle   time _____
Ladder run   time _____
Coin catches (10 tosses)
   Type of coin _____ outs _____ errors _____
Hot potato   no. of throws in 30 seconds _____
Wall ball   no. of catches in 30 seconds _____

For Further Information

Books

Converse All-Star Baseball: How to Play Like a Pro. New York, New York: John Wiley & Sons, 1997.

Frank Jobe & Diane Moynes, *Official Little League Fitness Guide*. New York, New York: Simon and Schuster, 1984.

Jerry Kasoff, *Baseball Just for Kids*. Englewood Cliffs, New Jersey: Grand Slam Press, 1996.

Ned McIntosh, *Little League Drills and Strategies*. Chicago: Contemporary Books, 1987.

Magazines

Junior Baseball
Sports Illustrated for Kids

Organizations

Babe Ruth Baseball/Softball
    www.baberuthleague.org
Frozen Ropes Training Centers
    www.frozenropes.com
Little League Baseball
    www.littleleague.com
National Strength & Conditioning Association
    www.nsca-lift.org
Pony Baseball/Softball
    www.pony.org

Index

About the Author

Jeffrey B. Fuerst has written nonfiction and fiction books, plays, TV shows, magazine articles, and Web site features for kids. He is the recipient of the Educational Press Distinguished Achievement Award. This is his first book for The Millbrook Press. Throughout his career, Fuerst, who lives in Hastings-on-Hudson, New York, with his wife and two children, has been a switch-hitting middle infielder.